A DAY IN THE LIFE OF A COMMUNITY SERVICE VEHICLE

A DAY IN THE LIFE
OF A FIRE TRUCK

by Nicole A. Mansfield

PEBBLE
a capstone imprint

Published by Pebble, an imprint of Capstone
1710 Roe Crest Drive, North Mankato, Minnesota 56003
capstonepub.com

Copyright © 2025 by Capstone. All rights reserved. No part of this publication may be reproduced in whole or in part, or stored in a retrieval system, or transmitted in any form or by any means, electronic, mechanical, photocopying, recording, or otherwise, without written permission of the publisher.

Library of Congress Cataloging-in-Publication Data is available on the Library of Congress website.
ISBN: 9780756586904 (hardcover)
ISBN: 9780756586850 (paperback)
ISBN: 9780756586867 (ebook PDF)

Summary: Look! A big, red fire truck zooms down the street. It is on its way to a fire. Going to a fire can be one part of a fire truck's day. But that's not all! From equipment checks to washing their trucks, find out how firefighters use these important vehicles from sunrise to sunset.

Editorial Credits
Editor: Carrie Sheely; Designer: Elyse White; Media Researcher: Jo Miller; Production Specialist: Tori Abraham

Image Credits
Alamy: Ivan Marc Sanchez, 5, STUDIO BONOBO, 18; Capstone: Karon Dubke, 8, 11; Getty Images: Alan Rubio, 9, Birzio, 15, John Coletti, 6, Mint Images, 19, Ocskaymark, 14, Petko Ninov, 7, 10, Sean Hannon, 17, tazytaz, 12; Shutterstock: EdBelkin, cover (front and back), Niko_V, 20 (stapler), Oleg Golovnev, 20 (paper), Olivier Le Queinec, 13, Tropper2000, 21

Any additional websites and resources referenced in this book are not maintained, authorized, or sponsored by Capstone. All product and company names are trademarks™ or registered® trademarks of their respective holders.

Printed in the United States   6316

TABLE OF CONTENTS

Emergency Vehicles 4

Sunrise Equipment Checks 6

An Afternoon Emergency! 12

Sundown at the Station 18

Make a Fire Truck Art Book 20

Glossary 22

Read More 23

Internet Sites 23

Index 24

About the Author 24

Words in **bold** are in the glossary.

EMERGENCY VEHICLES

Zoom! A big, red truck zips by. It has a long ladder on its roof. People hear its loud sirens. It is on its way to a fire.

Fire trucks are **emergency** vehicles. They help put out fires in our **communities**. Firefighters are workers who use fire trucks.

SUNRISE EQUIPMENT CHECKS

A fire truck's day begins before sunrise. The trucks are parked in a fire station. The fire station is never closed.

Firefighters check equipment on the trucks. They test the saws. Saws help cut openings in buildings. The openings may be cut to release smoke. Openings also help firefighters get into burning buildings fast!

Firefighters make sure each truck's water pump works. They check the pump **gauges**. They turn on bright lights. Firefighters test the sirens and horns too. Beep!

Next firefighters check a fire truck's **automated** aerial ladder. Up the ladder goes! Aerial ladders can be more than 100 feet (30 meters) tall. That's longer than a full-size basketball court!

It is a special day at the station. Students come for a field trip. The students get to sit up front in the **cabin**. The firefighters teach kids about fire safety. They learn about the important job of fire trucks.

AN AFTERNOON EMERGENCY!

Ring! In the afternoon, the fire station's alarm goes off! The truck leaves the station in under five minutes. The truck's sirens blast. The truck zooms down the street.

The fire truck arrives at the fire. Flames are coming from a tall building! The fire truck's heavy metal legs come down. They are called outriggers. These legs keep the truck planted on the ground.

A firefighter uses a joystick at the bottom of the ladder. The ladder goes up. Firefighters are in the ladder's bucket. Water sprays out of a nozzle attached to the bucket. *Whoosh!*

Soon the fire is out. The firefighters get their equipment. They carefully put it back in the truck.

bucket

As the truck is leaving, the firefighters get called to a nearby car crash. The truck blocks traffic lanes. It helps keep workers at the scene safe.

SUNDOWN AT THE STATION

The sun is setting as the truck pulls back into the station. The tired firefighters put more **fuel** in the truck. The truck has its own pump at the fire station. Then firefighters wash the truck.

The trucks and the crew are at the station overnight. They will be ready for the next emergency. In the morning, a new crew will arrive.

19

MAKE A FIRE TRUCK ART BOOK

You learned a lot about what fire trucks do all day. Now, let's draw to show what you learned. Follow the directions to make an art book.

What You Need:

- 3–5 sheets of paper
- colored pencils
- stapler

What You Do:

1. On each sheet of paper, use colored pencils to draw a picture of one thing that fire trucks do.

2. Stack the papers on top of one another.

3. Staple the papers together down one side.

4. Share your story with your family and friends to show what you learned.

GLOSSARY

automate (aw-TOE-mayt)—to do a job using a machine

cabin (KA-buhn)—the part of a fire truck where firefighters sit

community (kuh-MYOO-nuh-tee)—a group of people who live in the same area

emergency (i-MUHR-juhn-see)—a sudden and dangerous situation that must be handled quickly

fuel (FYOO-uhl)—anything that can be burned to give off energy

gauge (GAYJ)—a dial or instrument used to measure something, such as an engine's temperature

READ MORE

Dickmann, Nancy. *Fire Trucks*. North Mankato, MN: Capstone, 2022.

Driscoll, Laura. *I Want to Be a Firefighter*. New York: Harper, 2022.

Peterson, Christy. *A Trip to the Fire Station with Sesame Street*. Minneapolis: Lerner Publications, 2022.

INTERNET SITES

Kiddle: Fire Engine Facts for Kids
kids.kiddle.co/Fire_engine

NFPA Kids: Explore a Truck
sparky.org/firetrucks

PBS LearningMedia: Fire Station Field Trip
tpt.pbslearningmedia.org/resource/89d8204a-c024
-4d33-938a-a0bb60789d9c/fire-station-field-trip

INDEX

alarms, 12

cabins, 10

car crashes, 16

field trips, 10

firefighters, 4, 7, 8, 9, 10, 14, 15, 16, 18, 19

fire stations, 6, 10, 12, 18, 19

gauges, 8

ladders, 4, 9, 14

lights, 8

pumps, 8, 18

saws, 7

sirens, 4, 8, 12

smoke, 7

ABOUT THE AUTHOR

Nicole Mansfield is a mother of three, a wife, and educator. She enjoys singing and leading church worship music every chance that she gets! She is passionate about eating well and exercising. Nicole lives in the great state of Texas with her military family.